Practical Strengths:
A CliftonStrengths© Guide to Everyday Ways

Parenting

By Jo Self

Practical Strengths

A CliftonStrengths© Guide to Everyday Ways

Parenting

By Jo Self

2021

Content Editor & Creative Partner
Rhonda Rosborough

For my son, O
who inspires me to become a better parent

I also hold the deepest gratitude for:

Rhonda

Friend, fellow coach, confidant and content editor. Her
curiosity is the best editor & teacher I could have

Eduardo, Jim, & Joe

This series is only a reality because of you

Anna, Arlene, Caroline, David, Gilda, Kathryn

For always believing in me

Samir

For introducing me to the world of strengths

Thomas

For your continuous mentoring, knowledge and insights

Carlos

For giving me the most wonderful gift ever: O

And finally, _Dr. Donald Clifton_, thank you for your vision
and belief in seeing what is right in people

And to _all the parents_ who shared their stories and gave
this book their personal touch!

CONTENT

Parenting is not a practice. It
is a daily learning experience.

Talents are naturally recurring patterns of thought, feeling, or behavior that can be productively applied

A strength is the ability to consistently provide near-perfect performance in a specific activity.

Talents, knowledge, and skills -- along with the time spent practicing, developing your skills, and building your knowledge base - combine to create your strengths.

- Gallup

Introduction

I fell in love with CliftonStrengths© way back in 2003. I was introduced to it when it was still known as StrengthsFinder by a dear friend, Samir Gupte. The moment I learned my top five talents, I was hooked. It was as if I had received a user's manual for myself! The words that had always failed me when trying to describe why I did what I did, or why I enjoyed something so much, were now laid out before me. It was life changing.

Over the years, whenever someone came to me for advice, the first thing I would ask was, "do you know your strengths?" I would immediately have them read, *Now, Discover Your Strengths*, and then have them come back to me. Knowing their top five allowed me to have a deeper understanding of who they were and who they had the potential to be. Eventually this passion led me to become one of the first Spanish-speaking Certified Gallup CliftonStrengths© coaches in 2015. It is not just a job - it's a calling.

When people ask me, "Why Strengths?" My answer is fairly simple. I believe that strengths are the short-cut glossary into the human psyche that allows us to build better relationships through better communication and greater compassion. At the end of the day, it's why we are and why we're here. I truly believe if we can just appreciate the depth of understanding these 34 talents can give us, we can improve our relationships immensely - from the most intimate to the community as a whole. Once you see yourself objectively, you have no choice but to do the same for others as well. It allows us grace with ourselves, and others, that we may not have otherwise.

While there are some amazing materials out there to help us understand our talents at a deeper level, I always felt there was a small piece missing. Much of what exists is helpful in the professional realm, but there was a void in the day-to-day use of our talents. And our talents are *always* with us. They may show up differently in our different roles (parent, sibling, employee, volunteer, etc), but they are a deeply ingrained part of us. This is what led me to decide to write this series.

By recognizing these 34 talents, and how they show up for you, you will build confidence naturally. For me, a lack of confidence is merely a symptom of a lack of self-awareness. I want you to see yourself in a positive light and understand just how much your talents guide and lead you through your daily life - from relationships to how you spend your free time and everything in between.

My hope is that this book sheds light on something you may have taken for granted. That you now see your talent as something special, something to be valued and something unique to *you*. Also, how you can now harness this talent to build a strength and how to recognize when it might be getting in the way.

In strength and love

1

Don't worry that children never listen to you. Worry that they are always watching you.

- Robert Fulghum

Quick Reference: Parenting

You can find shareable graphics for each of these talents on http://discoverjoself.com/resources

ACHIEVER®: You work hard and you set a great example for your kids that having goals gets things done. You also demonstrate balance and that goals aren't only work related, but include self-care, family and fun, too.

ACTIVATOR®: You are the cheerleader for your child if they fail to act on their own. Hands on learning is where you excel and may also help your child discover what they enjoy and where they excel, too.

ADAPTABILITY®: More than most, you roll with the constant variables present in family life. You are able to embrace all moments with calm and provide stability and reassurance when unexpected turns throw your children for a loop.

ANALYTICAL®: You help your child handle challenging situations by breaking it down into simpler, bite-size bits. Your cool head is helpful in emotional situations, while recognizing that emotions are necessary and healthy as well.

ARRANGER®: Parenting is not a linear activity and requires a lot of juggling – which makes you an expert. You love teamwork and your ability to organize means each family member understands their unique roles in the home.

BELIEF®: You are a parent who walks the talk. Your child has no doubts about what is important to you. You help your child to identify what is important to them; and while belief comes from core values, it is respectful of others and their views.

COMMAND®: You are a model of leadership especially in tough situations which require strength and calm. You show your child that being in charge is about confidence in one's self while respecting others.

COMMUNICATION®: Words matter and you, more than most, understand this. When talking to your child, use your words in a positive and encouraging manner. You can teach them the power of effective communication early on.

COMPETITION®: You love to measure yourself against others to consistently improve. You model this for your child in a healthy way, showing them that we are all excellent at something. You also guide them to be both good winners and gracious losers.

CONNECTEDNESS®: Your open mindset demonstrates to your child that we are all connected and affect each other in ways we may not even realize. They experience solidarity through you and have an appreciation for "the big picture."

CONSISTENCY®: Your family always knows what to expect because you set clear ground rules that are fair to everyone. Your children know what to expect of you in return thereby creating a trusting bond.

CONTEXT®: It comes naturally to you to record important memories for your child and maintain family traditions that will stick with them for years to come. You also share lessons you've learned and funny stories from your childhood, bonding with your child in a special way.

DELIBERATIVE®: Your ability to see obstacles, paired with your cautious approach, teaches your child to evaluate risks thoroughly. Your thoughtful actions translate into a caring and loving sense of protection for them.

DEVELOPER®: You are a natural encourager. You easily recognize your child's special abilities and help them grow at a pace that serves them best. You appreciate each unique stage of childhood enjoying fully what each has to offer.

DISCIPLINE®: The structure and routine you provide for your child reduces anxiety and stress. This is especially relevant relating to new experiences. You also recognize that your child may have their own systems. You help them refine, discovering what works best for them.

EMPATHY®: Your child always feels your understanding and warmth, knowing they are loved because you express your emotions and share them in a healthy way. You also help them to express themselves when they are feeling unsure or insecure.

FOCUS®: With so many activities vying for your child's attention, you teach them how to prioritize and focus on what's most important. Keep in mind, what is important for your child may differ from you.

FUTURISTIC®: As tomorrow seems so far away for most children, your talent for envisioning the future helps them see what is possible before they can. Remember to celebrate the present, and not skip too far forward, missing the sweet moments here and now.

HARMONY®: Your focus on a win-win outcome for all teaches your child great negotiating skills. It also helps them find solutions to conflicts with friends and classmates. You bring family together through consensus.

IDEATION®: Boredom won't last long in your house with your endless ways of creating fun and learning for your children – from what they play to what they eat. They love that they can bounce ideas off you and their imagination is valued.

INCLUDER®: You create a strong family unit where everyone is valued and feels like they belong. You are most likely to be the house where friends gather because of your welcoming nature.

INDIVIDUALIZATION®: You ensure that everyone is appreciated and celebrated for their special talents, personality and abilities. You help each child reach greatness through what they do best.

INPUT®: Your ability to collect useful information, resources and people serve your child well. Share what you are learning with them and find ways to aim this knowledge together.

INTELLECTION®: You need time to reflect; ensure your children know this is OK by being fully present with them when you are mentally charged. It also teaches them to respect boundaries and individual needs.

LEARNER®: You share your joy of learning with your child. Explore new worlds together through classes, books and experiences which you can reflect on together. When you discover a child's passion, foster it by exploring further.

MAXIMIZER®: You easily recognize the true potential of each family member and support them to be their best. Remember to allow them to develop at their pace. While you can see their potential, they may need time and reassurance to see it themselves.

POSITIVITY®: You easily put a smile on your child's face, especially when their day has been challenging. You help them see the silver lining in tough situations, compliment them on what they are doing well and bring them hope for a better tomorrow.

RELATOR®: You carve out plenty of one-on-one time with your child, creating special moments where you can bond and deepen the relationship. Dinners, playdates, outings or even just connecting before bed each night strengthen your bond.

RESPONSIBILITY®: You are a great example for your children of what it means to keep your word. Your word is your bond and when you promise to do something, you deliver. Reinforce that it's ok to set boundaries and that no is an acceptable answer; you don't have to do it all.

RESTORATIVE™: Problems don't frighten you. You love the challenge of solving them, which puts your child at ease. They know they can count on you to help them navigate difficult decisions and problems that arise.

SELF-ASSURANCE®: The confidence you have in yourself translates to having confidence in your children. This helps them see themselves as valued and loved. You demonstrate that trusting in your own abilities includes listening to the opinions and thoughts of others.

SIGNIFICANCE®: Not only do you want to be a great parent, you also want to leave a positive legacy for your children. This motivates you to be there when they need you and guide them on how they, too, can make a difference.

STRATEGIC®: When your child is struggling with decisions, your ability to see patterns and options provides the information they need to make a wise choice. You are a great sounding board for them to think out loud as well.

WOO®: You are a master of organizing playdates and opportunities for your child to connect with others. You set a great example on what social graces can do for a person and the doors it can open.

1ᒧ

The way we treat our children directly impacts what they believe about themselves

— Ariadne Britt

WHAT would HAPPEN if **we** studied what was *right* with people VERSUS what's *wrong* with people?

Don Clifton

Photo courtesy of Gallup, Inc. Used with permission.

HOW TO USE THIS BOOK

Obviously, your first thought is to read about your own talents. However, I hope you will share this book with others and use it to try and understand them a bit better as well.

Quick Reference (The "Twitter" statement)
This is a brief description to sum up the beauty of your talent. You can even find a meme for each one to share here: http://discoverjoself.com/resources

The Gallup Definition
This is how Gallup defines the talent at its best and what anyone with this talent will recognize.

Celebrate & Evaluate
Here you'll find four bullet points under each heading. *Celebrate*: I want you to see the amazing value your talent brings to the table. These are ways in which you shine. *Evaluate*: you'll find questions to ask yourself to help you harness your talent and be aware of when it might be hindering you instead of helping you.

The Description
The description is a brief paragraph on how this talent may shine as it pertains to parenting. It will also shed a small light on how it may hinder you, so you can begin to think about these aspects as well.

Coaching Questions
Here I have provided three questions for you to consider a bit more deeply. I encourage you to use the space in the book, or in your own journal, to reflect on these questions and try to recognize your talent in your own life.

Have fun. Explore. Talk about it with your friends and family. And, most of all, discover the power within YOU.

Making lists and getting things done makes my heart (and mind) happy! And in parenting, I have found so much joy in creating schedules and lists of activities for the whole family to do and accomplish every day! Achiever helps me challenge, engage and encourage my 9-year-old, Lucas, to learn the value and satisfaction of completing activities and tasks. It helps us define and be clear on what is meaningful to do. As a family, it helps us plan, make our dreams tangible, and stay focused and present in what we do. While I have learned not to over plan and add too many things to the lists (which made all of us crazy), the energy I get from my Achiever talent helps me be creative, intentional, and purposeful in deciding what and how to get things done and feel happy about it. Our to-do's take the form of colorful post-its, written sentences on a piece of paper, point competitions through the day or words on a white board. Understanding and using my strengths has made parenting "easier" and so much more fun! Parenting, however, has inspired me to use my strengths in a different, incredibly meaningful way.

Achiever®

The ACHIEVER® Parent

According to Gallup: People exceptionally talented in the Achiever theme work hard and possess a great deal of stamina. They take immense satisfaction in being busy and productive.

Celebrate:

- How goals drive you
- Your to-do lists
- Your ability to work hard
- How you get things done

Evaluate:

- Am I becoming a workaholic?
- Am I expecting the same intensity from others?
- Am I forgetting about self-care?
- Am I adding too many things to my list?

You have a fantastic ability to motivate yourself when it comes to getting things done; however, make sure your to-do list includes non-work-related items, making time for family and self-care. As a parent, you are a great role model for your children on the benefits of tenacity and hard work. You demonstrate that goals are a great way to focus your intensity and create success. Remember though, that not everyone is as driven as you are and has their own way of reaching their goals. Be sure to talk with your children and see what motivates them to move ahead and create their own successful outcomes. By doing so, you can help them set goals which are appropriate for them.

On the following page you can explore your strength. Write down your notes and thoughts and "sharpen the saw".

Sharpen your talent with these questions:

What are the common goals you share as a family?

How do you recognize your children's accomplishments?

How do you define achievement? How do your children define it?

Ryan H, USA

In combination with the rest of my top 5 (Maximizer, Individualization, Futuristic, Positivity), my Activator comes out mostly as motivation to not wait for someday. My kids know to look to me for reassurance of what could be when they need a push. For example, my oldest daughter, Amy, would often find me in the living room reading or doing some work, and would bring me her latest concern with the social minefield that is high school. She would lay out the situation and we'd talk. We'd go over pros and cons and all the "what ifs". She'd continue to poke and prod by throwing up obstacles. She knew that eventually the real me would burst onto the scene with a motivational pep talk to back up all the things we'd already talked about. She knew it was all true, but she was waiting for Tony Robbins to walk into the room. When I allowed myself to be the real me, let that Activator (mingled with my other talents) out, then she had what she needed. My other two children, Lauren and Brady look for my Activation too, but it comes out differently for them based on *their* top 5. I adjust to how they need to hear me.

Activator®

The ACTIVATOR® Parent

> *You are the cheerleader for your child if they fail to act on their own. Hands on learning is where you excel and may also help your child discover what they enjoy and where they excel, too.*

According to Gallup: People exceptionally talented in the Activator theme can make things happen by turning thoughts into action. They want to do things now, rather than simply talk about them.

Celebrate:

- Jumping in with no fear
- Your hands-on learning approach.
- Your ability to innovate.
- Asking "why not?" instead of "why?"

Evaluate:

- Am I rushing my decision?
- Do I act impulsively?
- Am I communicating my ideas clearly?
- Is my impatience warranted?

You are ready for anything and that includes keeping your kids moving toward action. You are a cheerleader for them through failure, knowing that hands-on learning and making mistakes provides valuable learning – more so than not trying at all. You easily practice a growth mindset and continually encourage your children to keep going and keep trying. Even though you can easily be spontaneous, remember that not all members of your household may feel the same. Recognize that your children may need more time to transition and allow for that cushion as you make your plans.

On the following page you can explore your strength. Write down your notes and thoughts and "sharpen the saw".

Sharpen your talent with these questions:

Where could your child use help getting started?
What can you and your child do together to learn something new?
How do I encourage my children to explore new ideas?

Stacy B, USA

I have two daughters with totally different personalities. My high Adaptability enables me to tailor my parenting style and interaction to each daughter as well as blend both together when needed. I provide a calm demeanor when situations or plans change, and this is especially important when a crisis or serious issue arises. Instead of being reactive, I am able to respond calmly and help them talk through what happened and guide them towards what they learned or should do. My adaptability strength helps build trust which makes them comfortable coming to me if they need help or get into trouble.

Where my Adaptability can sometimes become an issue is when my daughters - especially when younger - need structure. In terms of planning our days, they are sometimes uncomfortable providing input into what we should plan. My remedy, when needed, is to provide a high-level plan, or to give them limited choices as to what to do, in order for them not to feel overwhelmed.

Adaptability®

The ADAPTABILITY® Parent

> *More than most, you roll with the constant variables present in family life. You are able to embrace all moments with calm and provide stability and reassurance when unexpected turns throw your children for a loop.*

According to Gallup: People exceptionally talented in the Adaptability theme prefer to go with the flow. They tend to be "now" people who take things as they come and discover the future one day at a time.

Celebrate:

- How you 'go with the flow'
- Your spontaneous nature
- How you adjust seamlessly to new situations
- Your flexibility

Evaluate:

- Is this change necessary?
- Am I blindly following others?
- Is my flexibility preventing clarity or understanding?
- Does this situation require a solid decision?

Kids keep everyone on their toes because the environment is always changing. Lucky for your family, you are quite capable of handling those changes like a champ. You provide stability and calm when unexpected situations arise, and you think quickly on how to make the best of the circumstances. You are flexible with the different needs and desires of each family member; however, be sure you are meeting your needs as well and don't get lost in the shuffle. Your appreciation of the here and now keeps your child grounded and able to focus on what is most important in the moment, without worrying so much about the future or dwelling too much on the past.

On the following page you can explore your strength. Write down your notes and thoughts and "sharpen the saw".

Sharpen your talent with these questions:

In which ways do you adapt to your children's needs?

How do you help your children handle sudden changes?

When do you stick to your own plans versus going with the flow of others?

Sumarie D, S. Africa

My Analytical talent keeps me objective in the chaos that is parenting of toddlers. It helps me to figure out and understand why they behave a certain way in certain situations, why some things bother them and why some things scare them. I always have to remember though that they need to vent their emotions before we can get objective to get to the cause of the emotions.

I love it when my kid asks 'why?' It is the door to exploration, to understanding, to learning, and it is a journey that I love to take with them. Instead of giving them the answer, I ask 'why do you think?' and it is amazing to see their gears turning. I love the little question marks between his eyebrows until finally the celebratory smile breaks through and I know – he understands.

Analytical®

The ANALYTICAL® Parent

You help your child handle challenging situations by breaking it down into simpler, bite-size bits. Your cool head is helpful in emotional situations, while recognizing that emotions are necessary and healthy as well.

According to Gallup: People exceptionally talented in the Analytical theme search for reasons and causes. They have the ability to think about all of the factors that might affect a situation.

Celebrate:

- Your desire for the truth
- Your ability to ask the 'right' questions
- Your methodical decision-making process
- Your cool head in tough situations

Evaluate:

- Am I stuck in analysis paralysis?
- Am I more worried about being right than finding compromise?
- Am I considering the emotional impact – on myself and others?
- Are all these questions necessary?

You are the biggest ally in helping your children make the best choices. Your practical way of breaking down problems - or just making the best decision possible – helps them see all important factors when thinking through the situation at hand. And when emotions begin to fly, you can calmly listen and bring reason to light – all while recognizing that emotions are healthy and valid as part of the process. By setting an example of the kinds of questions to ask, you demonstrate a healthy approach to problem solving and teach your children a valuable life lesson in the process. Remember, when asking questions, to enter with a level of curiosity and wait for the answers. This ensures it doesn't end up feeling like an interrogation. Take your time, listen and work through the problem together.

On the following page you can explore your strength. Write down your notes and thoughts and "sharpen the saw".

Sharpen your talent with these questions:

What process do you use to help your children
tackle big problems?

How do you guide your children to discover their
own proof?

In what ways do you express emotion?

As a parent of two, I lean on Arranger to juggle around all the variables taking care of two toddlers. The kids can count on me to make plans and be flexible when changes need to be made. I'm always on top of everyone's schedule. During the week, I can be busy at work and still keep track of children's school events. I love making plans: children's after school classes, family plans for the weekends, etc. When I do, I take into consideration my husband and my own schedule; I won't miss the routine schedules like nap time or bedtime and am always ready for plan B if anything unexpected comes up.

I am self-conscious, though, that my spontaneous nature doesn't become an interruption for the kids. I've also learned to empathize my husband, the other parent's pain in my ever-changing plans and involve him in the process. There is never a dull day in parenting, Arranger gives me the superpower to be a cool mom juggling many balls - including curveballs!

Arranger®

The ARRANGER® Parent

Parenting is not a linear activity and requires a lot of juggling – which makes you an expert. You love teamwork and your ability to organize means each family member understands their unique roles in the home.

According to Gallup: People exceptionally talented in the Arranger theme can organize, but they also have a flexibility that complements this ability. They like to determine how all of the pieces and resources can be arranged for maximum productivity.

Celebrate:

- Your ability to multitask
- The drive to focus on multiple projects
- Your ability to simplify complex arrangements
- Your flexibility

Evaluate:

- Am I overscheduling myself or others?
- Do I lose focus by juggling too many balls at once?
- Do things fall through the cracks?
- Am I too controlling of others' schedules or routines?

Kids are great at throwing curveballs – with their schedules, their projects (due tomorrow!) and just a general lack of planning. That's where you come in. Not only do you enjoy multitasking, you thrive when there's a little pressure to get things done – it allows you to laser in on which balls you most need to juggle right now. Does that mean you love constant, last minute tasks? Not necessarily, but it does mean you can handle it with ease and grace. You are a master of keeping everyone on schedule and making sure most things don't fall through the cracks; fortunately, this isn't likely to happen much on your watch. Maintaining the family calendar as well as each member's role in keeping the household running smoothly comes easily to you. Your family likely appreciates the finesse with which you manage it all.

On the following page you can explore your strength. Write down your notes and thoughts and "sharpen the saw".

Sharpen your talent with these questions:

How do you prioritize your family among your many projects?

Which activities do you let your family run or control?

How do you organize household chores and responsibilities? Do you choose or is it a family decision?

Lara M, USA

Ever since I can remember values meant everything to me and I discovered that this embedded in my Belief. This talent blends perfectly with one of my core values, family. The day I decided to have a family was the day I realized my life's purpose: children. No matter what it takes I thrive to make my husband and daughters happy. Sometimes my Belief comes out as protective, worrisome and negative but it is never intentional.

I've raised my kids on the basis of my core values - acceptance, unconditional love, honesty, integrity and respect - without ever imposing it on them but showing them the importance of values through my actions. I believe it is not what you tell your children to do but rather living and being an example for them.

Whenever there were disagreements, I always had an explanation and reason. As a result, my kids grew up to be quite the persuaders. I believe I created an environment where they can deal with any challenge based on the values/beliefs that I have instilled in them. I live, love and work by my core values.

Belief®

The BELIEF® Parent

> *You are a parent who walks the talk. Your child has no doubts about what is important to you. You help your child to identify what is important to them; and while belief comes from core values, it is respectful of others and their views.*

According to Gallup: People exceptionally talented in the Belief theme have certain core values that are unchanging. Out of these values emerges a defined purpose for their lives.

Celebrate:

- Your deeply developed values
- Your sense of meaning and purpose
- Your altruistic nature
- Your strong sense of integrity

Evaluate:

- Am I too set in my ways?
- Am I open to others belief systems?
- Are my opinions too strong or too rigid?
- Am I not allowing for "grey areas"?

You are a bedrock of stability for your family because they know what you stand for and why. You show them the importance of having core values and a steadfast base from which to lead through life. Your children know what to expect from you, which means you build trust easily with them. You also understand that they are on their own journey. You listen to them carefully and help guide them as they clarify their own beliefs and values. You show them how to respect others who may believe differently. You help them see that most of us lead from positive intention and that our differences are an advantage.

On the following page you can explore your strength. Write down your notes and thoughts and "sharpen the saw".

How do you express or celebrate your family's passion or values?
How do you handle a difference in values or passions among family members?
How do you allow your child to explore other belief systems and practices?

Jan P, England

I like to think of my (high) Command as a sleeping partner. As a parent. I was in control and could step in at any time. It helped me have a relatively calm and patient approach. Even a food shop was an interesting exploration. What? Where? Look? Nudging imperatives and directional movement. But that clarity of language and instruction was also a pitfall. Sharp words would create tears without need. Learning to be gentler was a revelation. And learning a sensitivity toward the child's preferred approach helped me navigate clashes of wills by anticipating things that would cause friction.

As a result, I've been able to tune in to one child's focused and organized Achiever and the other's relaxed, detailed and questioning exploration of the world. As a child of a high Command parent myself, I've worked hard to be less sharp; to give my children room to try and fail without stepping in. And I loan my Command out to my children to explore ways they can step-in and step-up to make a difference to others and be brave in the choices they make. Our mantra: try it, what's the worst that could happen?

Command®

The COMMAND® Parent

> *You are a model of leadership especially in tough situations which require strength and calm. You show your child that being in charge is about confidence in one's self while respecting others.*

According to Gallup: People exceptionally talented in the Command theme have presence. They can take control of a situation and make decisions.

Celebrate:

- Your ability to take charge when needed
- How you keep cool in a crisis
- Your honest and candid nature
- Your willingness to confront tough situations

Evaluate:

- Am I being perceived as argumentative or forceful by others?
- Am I asking or am I tellIng?
- Do I take over even when not asked or I don't need to?
- Am I coming across as intimidating to others?

You are a wonderful example of leadership for your children. Showing up with clarity and direct answers to their questions. They can trust that you will always be forthright with them and know what to expect from you. When chaos ensues, you are there to provide the calm in the storm. From sibling rivalries to difficulties in school, you face each challenge head on to find the best solution. Since your Command can come across a bit heavy handed to others – especially sensitive children – be sure you are listening closely and acknowledging positive efforts. The best leaders are the strongest support behind their teams – and that includes family.

On the following page you can explore your strength. Write down your notes and thoughts and "sharpen the saw".

Sharpen your talent with these questions:

What words can you preface your thoughts and opinions with to soften them?

How do you give your child enough space to think and act on their own?

How are you modeling leadership for your family?

Debbie S, USA

I love words and communication. I am fascinated by the use of language. As a teacher of young children, I felt a priority to give children a vehicle to express their wants and needs. We would model, teach and use single words, picture symbols, sign language and even communication devices. All so that a child could use their words so that others understood what they wanted.

As a mom and teacher, I found myself saying to a crying, frustrated child, "let's calm down together" and then "use your words" to tell us what you want.

I find my Communication in use when I use language to create pictures for others to understand a concept or idea. I tell stories to connect to others and show others that I understand what they are trying to say. I find myself using analogies - a lot - and using language to help explain an idea or process.

Communication®

The COMMUNICATION® Parent

According to Gallup: People exceptionally talented in the Communication theme generally find it easy to put their thoughts into words. They are good conversationalists and presenters.

Celebrate:

- Your ability to tell a captivating story
- Your clear explanations
- Being a good sounding board for others
- Your verbal processing skills

Evaluate:

- Am I listening as much as I'm talking?
- Am I missing what others are saying because I'm planning what to say next?
- Am I being clear and concise?
- Am I repeating myself too much?

You are the keeper – and teller - of stories. You teach through them. You demonstrate examples of right and wrong through them. You use them to bond even more closely with your children by sharing your own experiences and adventures. Your children love to listen to you because you are an entertainer with your words. It's not just about talking though, you're also an excellent listener and know when lending an ear is more helpful than speaking up. You likely do a lot of your thinking out loud. Let your children know that just because it's been said, doesn't mean it requires immediate action. They'll appreciate this sounding board aspect. It helps to understand complex situations by talking it through with you before deciding what to do. And when it comes to explanations, do your best to keep it clear and concise. Sometimes simple is best.

On the following page you can explore your strength. Write down your notes and thoughts and "sharpen the saw".

What stories do you use to illustrate lessons for your children?
How do you adapt to your family's style of communication?
How do you encourage open and honest communication from your child?

Jamie L, USA

Competition helps me see my kids as individuals because I'm always looking for areas where they can win. Rather than trying to make them a "mini-me", I look for where they have energy, joy, and natural talent because these are the areas where they have the most potential for success.

Every time I meet someone, I investigate where they are stronger than me. Then I can win by either learning from them or partnering with them. As a parent, I use this talent to identify and hone my kids' natural talents. I can see where they thrive, and I push them to be the best they can be in that area. Ballet was my passion as a kid, but both of my kids detest it. My older daughter is an extraordinary artist, and my younger daughter is a hip-hop dance ingénue. At first, I'll admit I was disappointed to let go of the dream of seeing them dance on a stage in a tutu, but then my Competition realized they would never be great ballerinas. Instead, I found the best art and hip-hop programs. They will go so much further in the areas where they naturally excel.

Competition®

The COMPETITION® Parent

You love to measure yourself against others to consistently improve. You model this for your child in a healthy way, showing them that we are all excellent at something. You also guide them to be both good winners and gracious losers.

According to Gallup: People exceptionally talented in the Competition theme measure their progress against the performance of others. They strive to win first place and revel in contests.

Celebrate:

- How you embody the spirit of winning
- Winning together is as important as winning alone
- Your drive and tenacity that inspires
- Knowing where to set the bar

Evaluate:

- Am I being a sore loser?
- Is MY win becoming more important than OUR win?
- Am I setting the bar too high?
- Am I praising the effort, even if the outcome isn't as hoped?

There's no team more important than family. You know that when one of you wins, you all win. But life isn't just about winning. You demonstrate to your child that persistence - and even small improvements - are just as valuable. They see your drive in everything you do. This inspires them to be passionate about their goals as well. Your determination is a great example for them. You also model being both a gracious loser and winner. Be sure to set the bars appropriately for your child's abilities and push gently as they will improve at their own pace. And remember, even the smallest win deserves a celebration. It will motivate them to keep up the great work!

On the following page you can explore your strength. Write down your notes and thoughts and "sharpen the saw".

Sharpen your talent with these questions:

How do you celebrate the wins in your family?

How do you help your children measure their own success?

How do you recognize each child's individual success or growth?

Teri J, USA

I see my Connectedness at play with both my grandsons. I was there when they came into the world, but my feeling of connection to them came before that, when I saw them in dreams years before they were conceived. Connectedness allows me to see aspects of myself as well as their father and mother in their personalities. My biggest challenge is not holding on too tight and allowing them to decide how much time we spend together. We came up with a system for them to let me know when they are ready for us (their grandfather and me) to end the visit: my 12-year-old grandson tugs on his ear when we are making eye contact and that means, "I want to play with my friends, but I'd get in trouble saying that, so you know what to do." Oddly enough, having this secret signal makes me feel very connected to him, for having the honesty and safety to ask for what he wants. The best part of our connection is when they show me the latest skateboard move or the mural they put on the wall of a bedroom. I feel a beautiful bond with each boy in different ways.

Connectedness®

The CONNECTEDNESS® Parent

Your open mindset demonstrates to your child that we are all connected and affect each other in ways we may not even realize. They experience solidarity through you and have an appreciation for 'the big picture".

According to Gallup: People exceptionally talented in the Connectedness theme have faith in the links among all things. They believe there are few coincidences and that almost every event has meaning.

Celebrate:

- How you trust your inner wisdom
- Your natural compassion for all living things
- Your ability to be a bridge-builder by bringing people together
- Your desire to be a part of something bigger

Evaluate:

- Am I coming off as naive?
- Am I waiting for circumstances to be "just right" before taking action?
- Are my personal boundaries blurry?
- Am I leaving too many things to fate instead of making a decision?

Your children look up to you as someone who radiates calm wisdom. When something hasn't gone according to plan, you find the deeper why in what happened and move forward. You find blessings in the lessons and this demonstrates to your children a purpose beyond the surface. You're also likely to build a community around you and your family, celebrating different cultures and ways of living. You enjoy exposing your children to new ways of thinking and seeing the world. You believe in the importance of teaching them that we all have a purpose and a path. You believe in the collective good around you, even when others only see strife and trouble. You know sometimes you need a good "shake-up" to "shift-up"; meaning, some unpleasant circumstances can lead to us being better than before. You take challenges in stride knowing that the path before you is bright, even if you can't see it just yet. Your children benefit from this optimistic way of seeing the world believing they play a part in making it better.

On the following page you can explore your strength. Write down your notes and thoughts and "sharpen the saw".

Sharpen your talent with these questions:

What larger purpose do you and your family support?

How do you discuss the differences we see in the world with your family?

How do you help your children see the bigger picture?

Sylvia I, Lebanon

I learned I had the talent of Consistency when I did the Gallup test in April 2018. Going back through the years I remembered how fast I used to gain people's trust because of this talent, which later helped me in parenting my kids. Sometimes I believe that God chose me to be the mother of my two sons because of this special and rare talent.

My eldest son is almost 18 years old and has Autism. With time, I learned that the key to succeed in teaching any child with Autism and help him master any task or reach any target, is being consistent.

My younger son is now 16 years old. As a toddler he used to be a calm and smart observer and was very much attached to me. He worried and cared about his brother a lot, even though he was sometimes jealous because of my attention that was directed mostly to his brother. My Consistency helped him feel secure by the time he reached his teenage years, knowing that I will keep loving, caring and serving him and his brother equally - and consistently.

Consistency®

The CONSISTENCY® Parent

According to Gallup: People exceptionally talented in the Consistency theme are keenly aware of the need to treat people the same. They crave stable routines and clear rules and procedures that everyone can follow.

Celebrate:

- Your clear expectations
- Your fairness
- How you treat others equally
- Your ability to set clear boundaries

Evaluate:

- Am I more concerned with rules than people?
- Are rigid expectations prioritized over responding to the needs of others?
- Am I enforcing rather than discussing or understanding?
- Is my way the only way?

"It's not fair!" Every home has heard this phrase at some point from their children. However, you know just how to come to the rescue better than most. You listen to their frustration and then find a solution that will create a sense of justice for them. You also set clear expectations and boundaries in the home. Each person knows their role and what is expected of them. This creates an innate sense of security and trust for your family. Since you may not give special treatment in the interest of fairness, be sure to always take a moment to praise each family member. You can even take it a step further by asking them how they would like to be praised. Rewarding the positive will build even deeper trust and understanding, leading to a happier home overall.

On the following page you can explore your strength. Write down your notes and thoughts and "sharpen the saw".

How have you involved the whole family to establish "house rules"?

What considerations helped you to set clear and just expectations for your children - according to their ages?

How do you balance your expectations with each child's individual needs?

Kathryn S, USA

My Context manifests most frequently with my daughter when she asks me a question about history – hers, ours, or worldwide – or how things work. I want to give her ALL the information – facts, perspectives, background and variations. Of course, she was wanting a simple answer and I'm giving her a lecture! She often latches onto something I've just said, asking another question, and I have to fight the urge to demand that she stay focused and let me finish. Now that I know this about myself, I'm getting better at letting her direct the conversation wherever her curiosity goes. My love for the background also means that I am the keeper of her history. I have saved so much of her past – from her first outfit, a lock of her baby hair, early art projects, samples of her handwriting at various stages and thousands of photographs. I love these objects, but I am saving them for her, so that one day she might look at them and know something of how she came to be who she becomes.

Context®

The CONTEXT® Parent

> *It comes naturally to you to record important memories for your child and maintain family traditions that will stick with them for years to come. You also share lessons you've learned and funny stories from your childhood, bonding with your child in a special way.*

According to Gallup: People exceptionally talented in the Context theme enjoy thinking about the past. They understand the present by researching its history.

Celebrate:

- That you have a relevant, historical perspective
- Your love for the backstory
- Learning from past mistakes
- Respecting your predecessors or elders

Evaluate:

- Am I too focused on the past?
- Am I holding a grudge?
- Questioning the perspectives without trust?
- Am I resisting change?

"I remember when" is likely a common phrase around your house. You love pulling up memories of your kids when they were younger and showing them how far they've come. You might even have a special scrapbook or memory box that you pull out occasionally to remind yourself how far you've come as well. In addition to the memories, you have a keen way of finding the backstory to situations and problems and use the information to help your children find their way forward by knowing the root of the cause. You also show them the path which has been laid out by previous generations, learning through their lessons as a way to not repeat their mistakes. And speaking of mistakes, be careful not to hold grudges when your children mess up. It's how they learn. And what they learn now will serve them as they grow.

On the following page you can explore your strength. Write down your notes and thoughts and "sharpen the saw".

Sharpen your talent with these questions:

How are you sharing your memories in a positive, constructive way?

How do you shine a positive light on the past to move toward the future?

What activities do you do with your children to preserve/document their family memories?

Deliberative is about recognizing potential risk. When raising kids, especially boys the risks can be terrifying. Where I saw Deliberative play out the most was with my youngest son. He has always had a strong will that have created many battles from a young age. Finally, around age five I realized he needed to understand the consequences of his choices. I would hold out my left hand and say, "If you choose this action, this is what's going to happen." Then hold out my right hand and tell him the second option and the consequence. Then I told him the choice was his as well as the consequences of his choice. The crowning moment was when I observed him looking at his hands and saying to himself, "I need to make the right choice." Now as a young man he thinks through his options and considers the potential consequences. When he's not sure of the options or consequences he seeks advise and sometimes even from his mom!

Deliberative®

The DELIBERATIVE® Parent

> *Your ability to see obstacles, paired with your cautious approach, teaches your child to evaluate risks thoroughly. Your thoughtful actions translate into a caring and loving sense of protection for them.*

According to Gallup: People exceptionally talented in the Deliberative theme are best described by the serious care they take in making decisions or choices. They anticipate obstacles.

Celebrate:

- Your vigilance
- Your perspective from multiple points of view
- Your conscientiousness
- You measure risk carefully and move forward accordingly

Evaluate:

- Am I too afraid of making the wrong decision?
- Am I playing Devil's Advocate just to be contrary?
- Am I holding others back with my cautiousness?
- Am I unwilling to trust decisions to others?

You are a model guardian for your children. You help them navigate their decision making by understanding the consequences of each action taken. While you can certainly help them see all the potential risks, you can also help them see the rewards. You also understand that some lessons must be learned on their own. This can be painful for you; no one likes to see their children hurt or suffer. However, you steadfastly stand by their side and catch them when they fall. Once the dust has settled, you explore options together to see how they might be more successful next time. Your family knows that your consideration of every detail is one of the ways you protect them and love them. They trust that you have their best intentions at heart and proceed accordingly knowing fully what lies ahead.

On the following page you can explore your strength. Write down your notes and thoughts and "sharpen the saw".

How can you help your child spot the obstacles in their plans?

What can you do to ensure you aren't holding back your child from making mistakes?

How am I giving my children the opportunity to act even if I don't agree with them?

Helen S, England

Moving through the stages of life can be daunting for both parent and child. I always related everything to confidence circles. To develop holistically you must be physically, intellectually, emotionally, and socially engaged. Keeping this in mind, when a new situation arose, I would have my child lie down on a big sheet of paper, something like old wallpaper would do. Then I would draw a big circle around them. Next, we would look at the potential new experience and work out ways of jumping out of the circle to make it bigger. It might feel really daunting to take a leap, but when you do, your energy levels are huge and the circle becomes even bigger - hence greater confidence. Some challenges I've had are always looking for ways to move kids forward and getting drained when things don't go to plan or other kids reach stages before mine! Be aware of comparisons. Also, when helping other mums move their kids forward and seeing my child is not quite ready, I need to accept it and not compete. Each kid is on their own unique journey and will reach their potential when they're meant to.

Developer®

The DEVELOPER® Parent

> *You are a natural encourager. You easily recognize your child's special abilities and help them grow at a pace that serves them best. You appreciate each unique stage of childhood enjoying fully what each has to offer.*

According to Gallup: People exceptionally talented in the Developer theme recognize and cultivate the potential in others. They spot the signs of each small improvement and derive satisfaction from evidence of progress.

Celebrate:

- Your dedication to progress
- Your talent spotting skills
- Your patience
- Your belief in the potential of others

Evaluate:

- Are we making progress?
- Is this worthy of my time?
- Is the other person interested in developing themselves?
- Am I pushing too hard?

You don't only enjoy each stage of your child's development, you celebrate it as well, thus giving your child pride and confidence in their abilities. You are a natural at spotting potential and then nurturing it. Even small signals of progress are worthy of recognition from you. While you see potential everywhere, ensure that your child feels the same. If they seem frustrated or less interested than you are, then maybe now isn't the time and it can be re-visited at a later date. You have the patience to let your child develop at their pace. Let your enthusiasm be a positive influence rather than a detractor. In the end, having a parent for a cheerleader is something your child will appreciate and love.

On the following page you can explore your strength. Write down your notes and thoughts and "sharpen the saw".

How do you celebrate each stage of development with your child?
How do you recognize when your child is ready to move up to the next level of their potential?
How can you give your child space if they aren't ready for the next level or stage?

Manish P, India

My daughter is a Dentist & a Gold Medalist scholar. I introduced Gallup Strengths to her soon after I certified as a coach and she was the first person I coached. I helped her align her entire course curriculum with her top 5 strengths - her Discipline at #2 was thrilled with the help. Other areas where I feel I influenced her are: she is never late for anything; she loves planners & the idea of a regular structure/rhythm; and her color coded progress bars on a chart pasted on her wall.

Having Discipline is not always good news for me or for people around me. I expect order, dislike tardiness and my organisation can intimidate others. None of that gets in the way of me parenting my daughter because she has a higher sense of Discipline. We only think differently when her priorities are different.

I wholeheartedly believe that embracing one's strengths results in not just creating huge effectiveness in one's life but also in influencing another person's life. As Josh Billings said in his quote: "To bring up a child in the way he should go, travel that way yourself once in a while."

Discipline®

The DISCIPLINE® Parent

> *The structure and routine you provide for your child reduces anxiety and stress. This is especially relevant relating to new experiences. You also recognize that your child may have their own systems. You help them refine, discovering what works best for them.*

According to Gallup: People exceptionally talented in the Discipline theme enjoy routine and structure. Their world is best described by the order they create.

Celebrate:

- How you easily break down big tasks
- Your ease with efficiency
- Your attention to detail
- Your ability to maintain a routine or schedule

Evaluate:

- Am I too rigid with others?
- Am I willing to be flexible when necessary?
- Am I too hard on others with their inattention to detail?
- Am I unwilling to change?

Children need routine and boundaries. You are naturally gifted to do this. Your children know how to tackle the big tasks because you break them down into easy, manageable steps. You consistently model how to work smarter, not harder; this helps them immensely in school and in life. While not every child may easily fall into a routine, the limits you set help them feel safe. Be mindful that what "organized" looks like to you, might look very different for them. Respecting their own way of creating routine and organization allows them to express themselves in the way they feel most comfortable. Also, remember that often the outcome is more important than the "how". Step back and ensure that your child is able to grow by thinking through the process for themselves. This will give them higher confidence in their abilities for the future.

On the following page you can explore your strength. Write down your notes and thoughts and "sharpen the saw".

How can you help your child develop their own routines?
How can you adapt your own routines to your child's needs?
What can you do to ensure you focus on the big picture over the minute details?

Empathy has been a 'superpower' of mine since before I can remember. As a parent, it allows me to be acutely in-tune with my three children and help them to feel all of the big things they as humans feel yet might not quite understand. Because I have an easy time expressing (most!) of my emotions, and care so deeply for others, it models for them how important it is to be open and honest about the way our bodies naturally respond and allow others to do the same. Something I do have to be aware of is to allow them to express or explain what it is they are going through and pulling in a few of my other top strengths to utilize healthy communication and patience. Since much of the time I can name (and even feel!) what they are experiencing, I have to pause and allow them to put it into their own words or signals so they are able to work through the process without me stepping in to call it something that might not be accurate for them personally. Empathy has truly been a gift to me throughout my life, and especially so within the framework of being a coach AND a mama.

Empathy®

The EMPATHY® Parent

According to Gallup: People exceptionally talented in the Empathy theme can sense other people's feelings by imagining themselves in others' lives or situations.

Celebrate:

- Feeling what others are feeling
- How you can "read a room"
- Expressing your emotions with ease
- Your kindness

Evaluate:

- Am I taking on the feelings of others too personally?
- Do I express my feelings adequately and appropriately?
- Am I being taken advantage of by others?
- Do I have clear boundaries?

Your family and children value how well they feel you understand them. They know that your love for them is deep and true. Your child is especially lucky as you will allow them to express whatever feeling they need to let out, as you know all too well how important that is. While others see you as sometimes too sensitive, be sure you let them know that you appreciate the freedom to express your emotions. This helps you recognize the emotion for what it is more quickly and work through it in a healthy manner, especially through painful times. You know what your child needs before they tell you. This means you are able to support them in a way they may not have been able to express themselves. Practice creating boundaries so that the energy of others is not completely absorbed, thereby maintaining a healthy balance.

On the following page you can explore your strength. Write down your notes and thoughts and "sharpen the saw".

Sharpen your talent with these questions:

How do you model healthy expression of emotion for your child?
How do you keep from being too permissive with your child to save their feelings?
What are your boundaries and how do you communicate them?

Lori R, USA

Focus calls me to set intentions in my parenting. My focus helps me identify what is important, such as core values and ways of being that anchor our family. And in that, focus helps me to push away the noise that gets in the way of focusing on those ways of being.

For me, my greatest intention as a parent is a question, "How do I want to be in this moment?" Focus helps me be in the moment despite the competing demands, whether that is taking the time to play tag with my kids, cultivate greater connection through noticing and honoring emotions, or doing another art project (while the laundry is left undone.)

I naturally lean toward accomplishing goals. Focus can help me redirect the "how" by focusing on the memories and connections of the moment. For example, when I am hiking with my kids, I have a natural tendency to prioritize the destination. However, Focus can help me reframe the goal and appreciate the "getting there" by stopping to play baby fox or noticing the fairy homes along the way. Those moments become the treasures of the memory.

Focus®

The FOCUS® Parent

According to Gallup: People exceptionally talented in the Discipline theme enjoy routine and structure. Their world is best described by the order they create.

Celebrate:

- Your ability to prioritize tasks
- Your targeted drive
- Your ability to zero-in on important details
- Your concentration superpower

Evaluate:

- Am I too focused on the details to see the big picture?
- Am I placing my priorities over the needs of others?
- Am I listening closely enough to others who might not have the same goals?
- Are my goals more important than people?

You are the one who clears the fog and chaos for your family, bringing clarity to any situation by honing-in on what's most important. When schedules are messy and plans seem to change on the fly, you can center in on the details and minimize any extraneous information. This makes you an amazing decision maker and shows your children how to develop their attention to detail in the process. You also understand what it means to be "in the zone". This means, when your child is in their zone, you are more likely to give them the time and space they need rather than rush them along. While you are trying to keep everyone on target, try not to get so caught up in the achieving the goal that you miss being in the moment or step on some feelings along the way. Take a moment to connect with each family member to see what's high on their list of things to do and help them decide the best way to prioritize by what makes sense for them.

On the following page you can explore your strength. Write down your notes and thoughts and "sharpen the saw".

Sharpen your talent with these questions:

How do you balance your own priorities with those
of your family?

How do you prioritize the emotional connection
between you and your children?

When are you "in the zone"? When are your
children in theirs?

Florence H, France

My Futuristic shows up mostly about being open to whatever projects my children may want to take on or dream about. I have 3 teenage daughters and of course this is the time where they begin to think about what comes next, study-wise.

I try to combine my talent theme and my experience to help them imagine what professional fields may actually look and feel like; and I believe this nurtures their own thinking.

I notice that I do tend to be a few steps ahead as to where we might go; what we might do, etc. - usually weeks, quite often months and sometimes even further. For me as a parent there are always many possibilities ahead ... I try hard to not put all these thoughts out in the open to my kids about « tomorrow » as I sense this could create added uncertainty; especially in the current context, or maybe causing disappointment when a vivid project ends up not materializing.

Futuristic®

The FUTURISTIC® Parent

As tomorrow seems so far away for most children, your talent for envisioning the future helps them see what is possible before they can. Remember to celebrate the present, and not skip too far forward, missing the sweet moments here and now.

According to Gallup: People exceptionally talented in the Futuristic theme are inspired by the future and what could be. They energize others with their visions of the future.

Celebrate:

- Your creativity and imagination
- Your vision for a better tomorrow
- The ability to see possibility instead of roadblocks
- Your ability to dream big

Evaluate:

- Am I appreciating the here and now?
- Am I being realistic with my vision of the future?
- Am I remembering to say thank you or appreciate current efforts?
- Am I co-creating with others or am I telling others how it should be?

Ah, the possibilities! It's so much fun wondering "what if?" with your kids. Listening to the dreams they have, what they want to be when they grow up, what they think the future looks like – you soak it all up. They love that their imaginations can run wild with you. You encourage them to explore all avenues and what could be. Try not to be too preoccupied planning and preparing for their future. There are plenty of sweet moments in the here and now to celebrate along the way. And remember, a child's idea of the future may only be next month, so be sure to adjust to where they are now and how far they can see ahead. With you by their side and a belief in their possibilities, they'll dream bigger and go further.

On the following page you can explore your strength. Write down your notes and thoughts and "sharpen the saw".

How do you talk about the future with your children? Is it positive? Daydreams? With expectations?

How do you keep your own visions of the future in check in order to listen to what your child is imagining?

How do you celebrate the day-to-day moments?

Gilda Y, Lebanon

People with Harmony are always rumored to have wind chimes in their homes. Spoiler alert! I'm guilty for having a couple swinging around on my balcony. One of the main moods I thrive to create in my home is peace and based on various encounters and compliments, I believe I have succeeded.

When it comes to parenting, I tend to lean toward teaching my kids to be diplomatic with their friends and reliant on the school administration to settle their arguments rather than being unproductively confrontational. Using my Harmony, I have always been able to settle the arguments by offering them a clear view of both sides. As they grew older, I came to realize they were mirroring my Harmony and were able to settle disputes in a calm and easy way. However, due to my sensitivity towards emotional unrest, I slowly began to realize how they would use my Harmony against me in order to get out of trouble. Although people love and enjoy the peace I offer, I am often criticized for my easy-going attitude that practices little discipline.

Harmony®

The HARMONY® Parent

According to Gallup: People exceptionally talented in the Harmony theme look for consensus. They don't enjoy conflict; rather, they seek areas of agreement.

Celebrate:

- Your calm and balanced nature
- Your ability to gain consensus
- Seeing reciprocity as a win-win and it's not always 50/50
- Your negotiating skills

Evaluate:

- Am I avoiding conflict?
- Am I just 'people pleasing'?
- Am I being truthful or evasive to keep the peace?
- Am I being indecisive?

Your natural negotiating skills come in handy when family members or your child and his friends have disagreements. You find a win-win for everyone, so they walk away feeling positive about the outcome. Be sure to voice your own desires as well; it's important that *all* voices are heard. Speaking up and being truthful about your own needs will go far in keeping the peace at home. This models for your child that everyone involved deserves to have their position - or opinion - considered. Your family appreciates the ease with which you approach the family as a team. Your ability to build consensus and divide family roles in a well-balanced way creates a happy home.

On the following page you can explore your strength. Write down your notes and thoughts and "sharpen the saw".

Sharpen your talent with these questions:

How do you bring your family together when there is conflict?
If you notice you are avoiding conflict, how can you lean into the discomfort and find consensus?
Around which values or activities does your family unite?

Sophie R-J, England

I am a homeschooling Mum of 2 and I use Ideation every day as a parent - it is my secret power to keep things running as smoothly as I can! My son has ASD, and my daughter shows signs of ADHD (which is hard to diagnose in girls) and they definitely keep me on my toes.

When my son is having a meltdown, I have to quickly come up with different ideas to bring him back down to calmness. Sometimes I have to change gears and think of a different approach – 5, 6 times (or sometimes more) - in a very short space of time, until I find the one that works with him in that particular meltdown.

Ideation is my homeschooling superpower too. As well as my own ideas, I love to collect the ideas of other mums who are doing an amazing job with their children. It either makes it into our planned learning or I will use them on the spot when things aren't going to plan. When school is in session, my daughter (or both of them) will lose concentration, and I often have to think on my feet. We will stop and do something else I have thought of on the spot, and then regroup later.

Ideation®

The IDEATION® Parent

> *Boredom won't last long in your house with your endless ways of creating fun and learning for your children – from what they play to what they eat. They love that they can bounce ideas off you and their imagination is valued.*

According to Gallup: People exceptionally talented in the Ideation theme are fascinated by ideas. They are able to find connections between seemingly disparate phenomena.

Celebrate:

- Your love of brainstorming
- Making connections others may overlook
- Your ability to innovate
- Asking "why not?" instead of "why?"

Evaluate:

- Are my ideas actionable?
- Do I change direction too fast?
- Am I delaying the end goal?
- Am I communicating my ideas effectively?

You have an energy about you which is passionate and creative. Ideas flow from you with ease and this means it would be challenging to be bored in your house. Your kids will love that you are always finding new ways to teach them and play with them. You aren't afraid of doing things a new way and that flexibility inspires creativity in the rest of the family. You see connections that others may overlook – where some only see dots with numbers on them, you see the bunny rabbit without even drawing a line. It's almost intuitive. Seeing these connections can help your children solve problems and come up with their own creative solutions. They may even see a cause and effect they hadn't considered when thinking through the consequences of their actions.

On the following page you can explore your strength. Write down your notes and thoughts and "sharpen the saw".

How do you encourage your children to solve problems creatively?

In which situations would you like to improve the way you communicate your ideas?

How do you "stay the path" when you've made plans and your family is counting on you?

Kelly W, Peru

For me, it is very easy to be the new parent in a group. I am always seeking unity and looking for something we can all connect on, often this appears in the form of a well-timed joke or the sharing of a delicious snack I brought for all to enjoy. Once the ice is broken and people are at ease, I realize my tendency is to quietly slip away from the group and help with whatever job needs to be done, sit with someone who is alone or check on what the children are doing.

As an Includer I get really uncomfortable if I see a child being left out or picked on. While I know it is best to assess the situation and see if the kids can work it out on their own before jumping in to "solve the problem", my first impulse is to stop the exclusive behavior and find common interests among the kids or ask if any of them have a funny story they want to tell. I love when everyone can laugh together.

Includer®

The INCLUDER® Parent

You create a strong family unit where everyone is valued and feels like they belong. You are most likely to be the house where friends gather because of your welcoming nature.

According to Gallup: People exceptionally talented in the Includer theme accept others. They show awareness of those who feel left out and make an effort to include

Celebrate:

- Your abilities as a natural team builder
- Making others feel at ease, especially new people
- Your acceptance of others as they are
- How you fight for or support the underdog

Evaluate:

- Am I being indecisive?
- Am I avoiding confrontation?
- Am I including the *right* people for the task at hand?
- Am I being overly generous?

Your home is where everyone likes to gather. People love being around you as you make everyone feel welcome. When your own child is feeling left out, you find ways to help them feel included. You might invite other friends over to play. Or perhaps you discover a new park or place to go where your child has the chance to make new friends. It's likely you make chores more fun around the house as well. You let each person choose the job they most prefer and let everyone pitch-in in their own way. Be careful about inviting all the kids over for a visit though. There may be a reason your child isn't interested in hanging out with certain people. It's best to let your child lead the way, while also modeling tolerance and acceptance of others. They'll appreciate the diversity amongst their peers by following your lead.

On the following page you can explore your strength. Write down your notes and thoughts and "sharpen the saw".

How do you get your child's input before inviting other kids over to your home?

How do you model inclusion and diversity for your child?

What games or systems do you have in place to include your family in making decisions?

Margareta T, S. Africa

My strength of Individualization came through very prominently in the parenting of my 2 boys, now young adults. From very early on, I noticed, and highlighted to each of them, to understand each other better, their individual differences in talents in say sports or other interests. I always taught them that they should try do their best in a talent. One might be better at ball skills whereas other may be better at math, for example. There were times that I did have to tone down my Individualization strength when it came to family rules such as sitting down to dinner together at a specific time. I encouraged their individuality in choosing their own favourite dish at least once a month that everyone should try. I was also 'accused' of always taking the others' side when I was only trying to explain to them to see it from the other's point of view; however, that has now stood them in very good stead through their university and early career. They now better understand and tolerate other people's differences. It takes many of us to make the world go round and we all contribute our own uniqueness to the table.

Individualization®

The INDIVIDUALIZATION® Parent

According to Gallup: People exceptionally talented in the Individualization theme are intrigued with the unique qualities of each person. They have a gift for figuring out how different people can work together productively

Celebrate:

- You celebrate the unique individuality and differences of each person
- How you make others feel special
- Recognizing all the factors which create the 'whole' person
- Your personalized attention

Evaluate:

- Is the group being sacrificed for the individual?
- Am I valuing potential over performance?
- Are the rules too flexible?
- Am I being too flexible – bending to the desires/needs of others?

You can pick the perfect gift for everyone in your family. Why? Because you pay attention. You have a way of not just seeing the uniqueness in each person, but you pay attention to the small details, habits, likes and dislikes as well. You also see potential in your children and will help them focus on that uniqueness – giving them power and confidence in their own ability. The way you love them helps them love themselves. As you recognize each family member's personal challenge, make sure the rules you set aren't bending one way for one person and the other way for someone else. While there is little room for "black and white" thinking in your world, the grey area could be confusing our children when it comes to boundaries and rules. Including the whole family in the creation of household policies and rules ensure that each voice is heard, and a democratic decision is made.

On the following page you can explore your strength. Write down your notes and thoughts and "sharpen the saw".

How do you show your child(ren) that they are special?

What are the boundaries or house rules that everyone must follow - no exceptions?

How do you bring your family together when each person has an idea for what they want to do, to eat, to watch on TV, etc?

Susan B, USA

I've always had a naturally inquisitive mind that craves information. Over the years, I collected and stored all sorts of information that I could hopefully share with others so that they could succeed. I had researched extensively to help one daughter write a resume and cover letter; and it recently came in handy again as my 20-year-old grandson now needed the same help. Of course, time had passed, so I needed to do more research to update my knowledge. The two experiences were quite different having developed my talent into a strength. With my daughter, I dumped way too much information. I had her write and rewrite until she titled one email: "The last one I hope!" This time I only covered the basics and sent my grandson off to write his own resume. He did a great job. I congratulated him *and* made only one suggestion. Neither of us was overwhelmed with all the possibilities of what to include.

Input®

The INPUT® Parent

> *Your ability to collect useful information, resources and people serves your child well. Share what you are learning with them and find ways to aim this knowledge together.*

According to Gallup: People exceptionally talented in the Input theme have a need to collect and archive. They may accumulate information, ideas, artifacts or even relationships.

Celebrate:

- Your resourcefulness
- Your desire to share information & resources
- Having the right information, at the right time, for the right person
- Your better than average memory

Evaluate:

- Am I asking too many questions?
- Am I applying what I'm learning?
- Am I collecting things which have a purpose?
- Am I oversharing information?

When your family needs help, you most assuredly have something in your bag of tricks to support them. It might be an article, a story, a wise saying. It might also be the overstuffed glove compartment or purse that always seems to have everything – a bit like Mary Poppins. You might also hold onto the many memories of childhood and as your child grows, those little souvenirs serve as reminders to each joyous moment. If holding on to those little items begins to look more like clutter, consider creating a photo scrapbook which will stir those memories without taking up so much space. As your child grows, you will thoroughly enjoy the journey of discovery right along with them, bringing new insights and resources to each experience.

On the following page you can explore your strength. Write down your notes and thoughts and "sharpen the saw".

Sharpen your talent with these questions:

In what ways do you encourage your child to research or discover on their own?
What is your management system for information or things?
How do you share what you know with your children?

When I understood my talent of Intellection, it was quite a game changer for me in work and in life as it has provided me with a powerful tool to accomplish tasks more effectively, productively and ask for help sooner. Although, I need to process information I can communicate this effectively and create a greater trust with others.

It is also a powerful tool when speaking to my children, even though they are adults, because they see me more authentically than when they were growing up. I am especially grateful that I can also share with my grandchildren how focusing on what we do well will encourage open dialogue and provide opportunity for them to flex their talents more effectively.

I can solve problems, develop an idea or understand another person's feelings - if I allow myself the space to think about the information I received. The result for me and others such as my children or grandchildren is that we interact more authentically and without misunderstandings because we openly communicate our needs and our expectations.

Intellection®

The INTELLECTION® Parent

You need time to reflect; ensure your children know this is OK by being fully present with them when you are mentally charged. It also teaches them to respect boundaries and individual needs.

According to Gallup: People exceptionally talented in the Intellection theme are characterized by their intellectual activity. They are introspective and appreciate intellectual discussions.

Celebrate:

- Your depth and profoundness for understanding
- Your philosopher's mindset
- Having deep, meaningful conversations
- Your ability to move slowly

Evaluate:

- Am I isolating myself?
- Am I thinking about the right things?
- Am I getting frustrated with others who move faster than I do?
- Am I building walls or emotional barriers to keep others at arm's length?

One of the benefits of your Intellection talent is a calmness and patience that comes with it. You easily provide a safe space for your family to say what needs to be said as you listen attentively and process what they are saying and feeling. You also hold space for yourself, knowing you need it to "charge your battery" in order to be fully present for your family. This is a great lesson around individual needs. You ask deep questions to get an even greater understanding of what they are going through and to help them find a path forward. You enjoy having philosophical conversations with your children and have fun exploring the "what ifs" of life. Those conversations create a close bond and let your children know there's no question too complex or too silly to ask you. When they do, you are likely to respond with a thoughtful commentary or opinion. Remember to have fun as well! Not all questions will lead to the meaning of life, but they will provide for keen insights to each of your family members and how they think.

On the following page you can explore your strength. Write down your notes and thoughts and "sharpen the saw".

How do you find space for yourself to think and reflect?
How do you include your children in the "big" conversations and philosophical questions?
How do you balance being intellectual with being emotional?

Rhonda R, USA

As Nana, some of my most treasured times are learning from my five grandchildren, ages three to nine. In summer, we have Nana's Camp where I plan activities and outings based on what they like to do as individuals and together as a group. I am open to new experiences and discoveries on these adventures - never quite knowing where we are going to end up and many times surprised at where we do end up. Each child takes my curiosity on a magical journey from one topic to the next! I listen closely to see the world through their eyes. My curiosity asks many questions to understand their different perspectives. I also remind myself that they may not enjoy the learning process as much as I do and that I need to meet them at their own pace. My Learner loves the simplicity in which they view the world - stripping away the complex to show me pure beauty, love, and laughter. Their excitement and continuous movement keep me in the present and allows my Learner to explore the playfulness, joy, and energy of each moment.

Learner®

The LEARNER® Parent

> *You share your joy of learning with your child. Explore new worlds together through classes, books and experiences which you can reflect on together. When you discover a child's passion, foster it by exploring further.*

According to Gallup: People exceptionally talented in the Learner theme have a great desire to learn and want to continuously improve. The process of learning, rather than the outcome, excites them.

Celebrate:

- Your curiosity about many things
- Your great perspective on a variety of subjects
- Your appreciation for different ways of learning
- Learning from your mistakes

Evaluate:

- Is this just curiosity or does it serve a purpose?
- Am I a know-it-all?
- Am I applying what I learn?
- Am I sharing and/or using my knowledge appropriately?

Having children is just one big opportunity to learn and you love it! Not only do you get to expand your knowledge, but you get to witness each new lesson your child is discovering. And when you discover together? That's pure magic. Remember to share what you learn with your child and pass on your knowledge. At the same time, tap into your own curiosity to learn more about them and their perspectives. When you discover a child's passion, help them to take it to the next level and explore it further together. Keep in mind that you have a lot of experience and knowledge, and what may be obvious to you, is still new for them. So, step back and learn something all over again - through their eyes - and you just might be surprised at what *they* teach *you*.

On the following page you can explore your strength. Write down your notes and thoughts and "sharpen the saw".

Sharpen your talent with these questions:

How do you engage your child's curiosity?

When your child asks a question, how do you decide between telling them what you know or going on a journey of discovery with them?

In what ways can you actively learn with your child?

Being a Maximizer parent has me always looking for the best in my kids and cheering them on to Play to Their Strengths! I'm not interested in fixing their weaknesses. Instead, on a regular basis, I sit down with them to evaluate their performance in school and extra-curricular activities then coach them toward excellence in the areas of their greatest strengths.

It's important for me to remember to pause and celebrate success. As a Maximizer parent, I can lean too far into my expectations for outstanding performance and leave my kids feeling as though I'm "nit-picking" their efforts. I've learned to inspire confidence, engage their strengths, celebrate success, and then later on, evaluate how to build on their success!

Maximizer®

The MAXIMIZER® Parent

> *You easily recognize the true potential of each family member and support them to be their best. Remember to allow them to develop at their pace. While you can see their potential, they may need time and reassurance to see it themselves.*

According to Gallup: People exceptionally talented in the Maximizer theme focus on strengths as a way to stimulate personal and group excellence. They seek to transform something strong into something superb.

Celebrate:

- Your dedication to excellence
- Preferring quality over quantity
- Your focus on strengths
- Your motivational manner

Evaluate:

- Am I being a perfectionist?
- Is the outcome realistic?
- Are my expectations too high?
- Am I mirroring excellence or only demanding it?

You easily recognize each family member's potential, and you are there to support them as they develop their unique strengths. Mirror this for them until they recognize it for themselves. Remember, this needs to be done at their pace, and not yours. They may have more difficulty seeing what you see. You also show your children how to work smarter, not harder. You help them explore the use of time, energy or costs to achieve what they want. This ensures a valuable return on that investment. You lean toward excellence. You have a deep desire to see your child develop to the best of their ability. For both reasons, you are a natural coach for your children, guiding them each step of the way.

On the following page you can explore your strength. Write down your notes and thoughts and "sharpen the saw".

Sharpen your talent with these questions:

How do you convey your excitement about your child's potential, yet let them set their own pace for personal success?
How comfortable are you letting your child make their own mistakes?
In which activities can you let your child take the lead, even if it takes more time or is less effective?

Joe D, USA

When my daughter was one year old, I was diagnosed with a non-cancerous, non-fatal brain tumor that has required 4 surgeries in her lifetime. On top of that, I had heart surgery when she was 6, followed shortly thereafter by her mother and me getting divorced, and then yet another change, moving to a new house.

My daughter, C, has a huge heart and is very kind, but these experiences have been difficult for both of us. My Positivity has helped both of us because, in spite of life's trials and tribulations, we both love to giggle at funny faces, smile at each other randomly, and have laughing fits as often as possible.

I always try to help her look on the bright side of things, practice positive self-talk and encourage her to have a positive outlook on life. My Positivity gives us strength. One way we do this is to create and give out thank you cards. They are usually 2x2 cards with an image on one side and a message of gratitude on the other. We love to give them out to people working at local stores and people that do work on our house. It brightens the day for all of us!

Positivity®

The POSITIVITY® Parent

You easily put a smile on your child's face, especially when their day has been challenging. You help them see the silver lining in tough situations, compliment them on what they are doing well and bring them hope for a better tomorrow.

According to Gallup: People exceptionally talented in the Positivity theme have contagious enthusiasm. They are upbeat and can get others excited about what they are going to do.

Celebrate:

- Your 'silver-lining' attitude
- The ability to visualize a positive outcome
- Your abundance of gratitude and compliments
- Your infectious smile

Evaluate:

- Am I avoiding problems?
- Am I being naive?
- Am I complimenting with sincerity?
- Am I actively seeking positive outcomes?

You are a person who knows that there are both blessings and lessons in life – and often the blessings come in the form of lessons. Your ability to be optimistic, even in difficult situations, brings a unique strength to your family. When your child is facing challenges, you often find humor or a silver-lining to lift their spirits and create hope. Your child will feel secure in what they do well, because you will naturally focus on their strengths and compliment them to reinforce it. Additionally, you recognize there is a time and a place to be the cheerleader versus knowing when your child needs to "feel" through the moment. You are excellent at reframing negative emotions and words to find the positive reference within. Where someone might see our child as stubborn, you see perseverance. With this ability to reframe, you often change others' perspectives for the positive as well.

On the following page you can explore your strength. Write down your notes and thoughts and "sharpen the saw".

How do you let your child experience negative feelings or beliefs?

How do you gauge those moments between offering encouragement and supportive silence?

How do you encourage and cheer your family toward success?

Jennifer V, USA

Having Relator, relationship drives every interaction with my kids. I'm always thinking, "What decision reinforces the relationship?" It might be helping to put away laundry when it should be bedtime or clearing my schedule to cheer for their afterschool soccer and volleyball games. Early on, I tried to parent with other people's strengths, but I learned to parent from my own. Now, my kids come home on time for curfew NOT because they fear punishment, but because they know how much I will worry if they are late. Focusing on "Relationship over Rules," helps my kids relate to me as a person who cares and helps me relate to them as people who understand their choices affect others. I also learned to be intentional about spending time with my kids. "I want to spend time with you. We can do anything you want, but I need some one-on-one time with just you." They don't lead from Relator, but they honor the fact that I do. The older they get, the stronger our connection grows. We have always prioritized trust, telling the truth and my daily saying, even when in a hurry, is "There's always time for a hug."

Relator®

The RELATOR® Parent

According to Gallup: People exceptionally talented in the Relator theme enjoy close relationships with others. They find deep satisfaction in working hard with friends to achieve a goal.

Celebrate:

- Your loyalty and trustworthiness
- Your values of honesty and authenticity
- Your close circle of friends
- How easily you build relationships

Evaluate:

- Am I isolating people?
- Do I appear closed off or aloof?
- Do I play favorites?
- Am I holding any grudges?

You value close relationships and deepening the bond you have with your child is a high-priority for you. Besides active experiences (games, outings, playing together), you also treasure the quiet moments snuggling, reading books, and daydreaming while watching clouds go by. Whatever time you spend is an investment in your relationship; one that will continue to evolve and expand as the years go by. You may get frustrated when other family members don't view these times together as important or prioritize them as you do. This may be because it comes easily for you and perhaps not for them. You are most likely the pivotal person in bringing family together—both near and far—to maintain a close bond. The ability to be 'you' among family and friends keeps you grounded. There is safety in familiarity.

On the following page you can explore your strength. Write down your notes and thoughts and "sharpen the saw".

Sharpen your talent with these questions:

How do you balance one-on-one time with each of your family members?

If a child breaks your trust, how do you help them earn it back?

How do you approach honesty with your children?

Vici B, England

My Responsibility flourishes as a parent. I strive to be the best parent possible. I work hard to provide the best opportunities for my son, whether that be the choice of school or dinner. Responsibility drives a standard; it means I always deliver on my promises and get a phenomenal amount done. It has also meant saying "yes" to far too many things. I can remember Joe playing football in the morning and driving him across the city to play a rugby game. Managing the various coaches and training sessions was an art, but we did it. Responsibility means I can lose my sense of humour and it has resulted in numerous arguments between us. We've argued about the need to complete all homework to a standard and on time. When we had too many things on, I would simply work harder to get everything done, I would micromanage things to ensure completion on time and to my standard. The greatest learning was when I reviewed Joe's Strengths and realised, I didn't need to micromanage him, he has talents that mean he can generate better solutions and outcomes than I can. We make a superb partnership and Strengths enabled that.

Responsibility®

The RESPONSIBILITY® Parent

According to Gallup: People exceptionally talented in the Responsibility theme take psychological ownership of what they say they will do. They are committed to stable values such as honesty and loyalty.

Celebrate:

- Your word is your bond
- People trust you
- Honoring your commitments
- Your accountability

Evaluate:

- Am I micromanaging?
- Do I have clear boundaries?
- Am I over-committed?
- When do I say no?

Your commitment to your family helps you to not only get things done, but to do it with their best interest at heart. When you make a promise, you keep it. When you are unable to, you will feel the regret or guilt more deeply than most. As a parent, you demonstrate the importance of setting boundaries, keeping your word and the possibility of saying "no" when necessary. Keep in mind that not everyone shares your level of commitment; though, they will likely come through for you because of the trust you have created and the example you set. Let your children take responsibility according to their abilities and age, especially when it comes to household chores. They'll appreciate having the choice and feel empowered.

On the following page you can explore your strength. Write down your notes and thoughts and "sharpen the saw".

How do you delegate different tasks among family members?
How do you clearly define your boundaries, so you know when to say 'yes' and when to say 'no'?
When and how do you give your children the space to accomplish something on their own?

Lenetta K, USA

My Restorative strength serves me well in parenting my many small children. Logic and reason have little meaning to them yet, so when there is a problem, I start with what needs fixed and work backwards. Is there something we can do to not even get in the situation in the first place? It is easy to forget how quickly they change and develop; and sometimes it's my methods that need fixing.

I have to be very careful that I don't focus only on the negative or what's wrong. I figure that we don't need to talk about what's right because … well … it's right! But my kids – indeed, nearly all people – bloom under positive reinforcement.

Finally, I am learning that not everything is a problem that needs resolving. Sometimes my kids just need to be heard, and I am slowly learning to discern the difference based on their reactions when I start making suggestions.

Restorative™

The RESTORATIVE™ Parent

According to Gallup: People exceptionally talented in the Restorative theme are adept at dealing with problems. They are good at figuring out what is wrong and resolving it.

Celebrate:

- How you solve problems
- The ease with which you handle difficult decisions
- Your commitment to doing things right
- Being solution-oriented

Evaluate:

- Is my focus more negative than positive?
- Am I fixated on problems rather than solutions?
- Am I being overly critical (of myself or others)?
- Is my viewpoint too narrow?

When your child has a problem that needs solving, you are the perfect person to help. You also foresee potential problems that may arise and can offer support on how to navigate through. Remember, part of growing up is learning from our mistakes, so be sure to give your child a little leeway. Be aware that others might see you as negative; just explain that what you really seek are solutions and not more problems. Just a little communication will go a long way in understanding this talent and its benefits for the family. Seeing multiple solutions to a problem is a great way to focus on the overall outcome instead of the process – a great model for your children to learn early.

On the following page you can explore your strength. Write down your notes and thoughts and "sharpen the saw".

How do you let your child know that you are there to listen and not to always solve the problem?
What are your systems or processes to help family members solve problems together?
How are you balancing careful critique with positive reinforcement?

Meg L-M, USA

I think of my Self-Assurance as having subtle influence on all my other parenting talents. I believe deeply in a growth-mindset approach to learning and with high Self-Assurance, I know my children can learn anything they dedicate themselves to.

That can show up in great ways for them - they get excited to try new things and tackle new challenges in life. My confidence in them gives them confidence in themselves; they don't see failure as final; they see it as the latest try. If I'm being honest, Self-Assurance can also show up as a drill sergeant, especially if a deadline or due date is involved. I do worry at times that my kids are anxious they'll disappoint me. I've learned to watch for their anxiety signs and to use a calmer (rather than authoritative) tone with them. I work to actively empathize and relate to their passions and to bolster them in times of doubt. As a mom of two daughters, I feel particular pressure to allow them to be themselves and to grow their own self-awareness so that they feel better able to stand on their own.

Self-Assurance®

The SELF-ASSURANCE® Parent

> *The confidence you have in yourself translates to having confidence in your children. This helps them see themselves as valued and loved. You demonstrate that trusting in your own abilities includes listening to the opinions and thoughts of others.*

According to Gallup: People exceptionally talented in the Self-Assurance theme feel confident in their ability to take risks and manage their own lives. They have an inner compass that gives them certainty in their decisions.

Celebrate:

- Your internal confidence
- Your ability to provide reassurance when others are in doubt
- Your steadiness in rocky situations
- The confidence you instill in others

Evaluate:

- Am I being dismissive of the opinions of others?
- Am I being stubborn?
- Am I being too authoritative?
- Am I impatient with others' insecurities?

Children test boundaries to establish their independence. Fortunately for them, you understand their desire to find their own way. You allow them the opportunities to discover their own inner compass and to make their own decisions. This doesn't mean that you don't set boundaries of your own for them. Yet, you are very proactive in discussing the consequences of their actions and decisions. You know they need to learn from their own mistakes, and you give them the space to do so. Of course, if things don't go according to plan, you are there to support and comfort them. Your strength of character also sets a good example and means your children are less likely to fall to peer pressure. They are aware of what's important to them and use their best judgment when temptation presents itself. By trusting their instincts, you inspire them to have confidence in themselves and to trust their inner voice.

On the following page you can explore your strength. Write down your notes and thoughts and "sharpen the saw".

How do you build confidence in your children?
How do you show your vulnerability to your children?
How do you allow your children to express their own opinions and explore their point of view with them?

Janelle J, USA

I want my children to be recognized for their unique strengths. I encourage them to know and develop their greatest selves and I applaud their successes in a more structured way than other parents. As my daughter approaches the beginning of high school, I have asked her to think about her graduation day.

What does she dream she would have experienced and accomplished? What will fill her with pride? What does she need to do now to make it happen?

The risk of a Significance strength in parenting is that I might unintentionally push my kids to achieve more, or differently, than they want. I am cautious not to do this, but I do still need to remind myself sometimes. I genuinely want them to be their unique selves and be the absolute best they can be. Whether my children strongly identify with Significance or not, they will demonstrate more of it their entire lives because it is a strong part of me as their Mom.

Significance®

The SIGNIFICANCE® Parent

Not only do you want to be a great parent, you also want to leave a positive legacy for your children. This motivates you to be there when they need you and guide them on how they, too, can make a difference.

According to Gallup: People exceptionally talented in the Significance theme want to make a big impact. They are independent and prioritize projects based on how much influence they will have on their organization or people around them.

Celebrate:

- Your free and independent spirit
- Your desire to make a positive difference
- Your drive to succeed
- Your comfort in the spotlight

Evaluate:

- Am I seeking recognition for the right things?
- Do I have a healthy balance between emotional and material success?
- Do I push others into the spotlight even if they are uncomfortable?
- Does my network serve a purpose or am I just "rubbing elbows"?

Because you are driven by purpose, you are a natural to inspire your children to think big and beyond themselves. While you may enjoy the spotlight, you may be just as content to see the spotlight shine on your family. You have an internal drive to leave the world better than when you entered it. What better legacy to leave behind than confident children who have found their own direction in life? You may also desire material things or hobnobbing with certain social circles. However, your deepest satisfaction comes from seeing that what you do or say has a positive impact on those around you - and the larger the circle the better. Remember your child may be more focused on a smaller reach. Join them on their journey and help them to make their own dreams come true.

On the following page you can explore your strength. Write down your notes and thoughts and "sharpen the saw".

Sharpen your talent with these questions:

How do you share the stage with your children?
How often do you have a family conversation around a family purpose or mission?
How do you celebrate both the small moments and the big ones?

Donna G, USA

Parenting with Strategic is a bit of a balancing act for me. I instinctively see patterns and options. I also see obstacles, and instinctively want to protect my children from disappointment or frustration. Yet I know sharing obstacles might quash or dampen their enthusiasm, creative thinking and aspirations.

To build trust with my children, I created opportunities to share my own decision-making process. I learned to be more open and to be a good sounding board. As a single mother of 4 young children, I had to intentionally create opportunities for conversations: while alone in the car, at the dinner table and late-night talks cuddled up on the bed. I helped my "dreamer" see possible pitfalls without squelching his vision. And helped the "worrier" quell her fears by listing potential obstacles and guiding her in a plan to manage or overcome them. When my children were "stuck" we found an alternate route through gentle questioning, engaged listening and prompting them to ask "what if" questions. Although tempted to smooth the way, I learned to listen. Each child found their own path and my role was to be the gentle guide.

Strategic®

The STRATEGIC® Parent

> *When your child is struggling with decisions, your ability to see patterns and options provides the information they need to make a wise choice. You are a great sounding board for them to think out loud as well.*

According to Gallup: People exceptionally talented in the Strategic theme create alternative ways to proceed. Faced with any given scenario, they can quickly spot the relevant patterns and issues.

Celebrate:

- How plan B is just the beginning for you
- You see patterns that others don't
- Your seemingly intuitive nature
- Your ability to see the "big picture"

Evaluate:

- Have I thought this through?
- Am I making the best choice?
- Am I considering others' opinions?
- Am I communicating my idea clearly?

Since every child is different and knowing that there are multiple ways to get to a desired outcome, you are open and excited to see how each child accomplishes the task at hand. Your children enjoy that you are an explorer and seek new ways to do activities. This demonstrates the power of asking "what if?" and the amazing things that can happen when we do. When faced with challenges, your family knows they can count on you to come up with several options on how to resolve it. When tackling a goal or looking for a solution, ensure that all who are affected by the decision have had a chance to share their thoughts. The fact that you can see the "big picture" means giving perspective to the situation; you are also more likely to care about "winning the war over winning a battle".

On the following page you can explore your strength. Write down your notes and thoughts and "sharpen the saw".

Sharpen your talent with these questions:

How do you help your children sort through their options?
What decision making process do you use with your children?
When things don't go according to plan, how do you and your family adjust?

Alicia S, USA

As it does to all areas of my life, my high WOO strength has brought energy and enthusiasm to my parenting over the years. Whether it was rolling around on the floor with my toddlers, planning playdates and parties, or listening to the latest rap music with my teens, I bring fun to being a mom. Although with my WOO, I have to make sure to balance discipline with play.

Though I was a performer from a young age and loved attention, it became quite clear early on, that I had to have a very different set of expectations for my two boys. I have learned how to modulate my social energy when in public with them and shift my expectations of what they "should" enjoy or participate in. The hardest thing for me to remember is that they do not like attention and get embarrassed easily! They are very generous with the reminders though – "No Mom, you can't chaperone my school dance because I know you will actually dance." Or "Mom, can we please get in and out of the grocery store without you making a new friend?" Fortunately, my WOO helps me receive the feedback easily since I don't take myself too seriously!

WOO®

The WOO® Parent

You are a master of organizing playdates and opportunities for your child to connect with others. You set a great example on what social graces can do for a person and the doors it can open.

According to Gallup: People exceptionally talented in the WOO theme love the challenge of meeting new people and winning them over. They derive satisfaction from breaking the ice and making a connection with someone.

Celebrate:

- Your ability to make everyone feel at home
- Your outgoing nature
- How you start conversations with ease
- You make socializing look easy

Evaluate:

- Am I coming off as shallow?
- Am I showing genuine interest in those I'm connecting with?
- Am I overshadowing others around me?
- Is my energy matching the room?

New home, new school, new activities? No worries! Your family knows that with you by their side, they will make friends in each new place in no time. Not only will you make new friends easily, you will also have playdates and invitations to your home organized in the blink of an eye. While you bring great energy to any situation, be sure your family is at the same level. They may not feel at ease with everyone as quickly as you do. Give them time and present opportunities at a level and speed comfortable for them. Your home is likely a gathering place for your children's friends as you make everyone feel welcome and at ease. You'll also show your child how to network easily and demonstrate social grace in a way that only you can. When they are sure how to start a conversation, you'll be there with tips and tricks to facilitate the process.

On the following page you can explore your strength. Write down your notes and thoughts and "sharpen the saw".

If your child is shy or introverted, how do you help them integrate socially?
How do you balance the attention you give your child with the attention you give others?
How do you help your child make new friends or find comfort in new situations?

Final Thoughts

I hope you found the information in this book useful. For my own part, knowing my strengths has helped me recognize those of my child – and we are definitely not alike! Knowing that we all have personalities and talents different from one another has allowed me to see my child for who he is and I now reconcile those differences in our personalities. Sometimes, as parents, we subconsciously treat our children as tiny versions of ourselves rather than seeing them for who they are.

For example, I have Activator and I can be very impatient as well as super spontaneous. O, on the other hand, requires time to transition from activity to activity and is less likely to enjoy my "in the moment" decisions. Meanwhile, his high Competition (based on StrengthsExplorer for kids) is challenging for me as I am not competitive in the slightest. But recognizing these talents in one another helps us to find some middle ground and a place of understanding.

I fully confess I am not an expert in parenting; but I do believe if we harness the power of our talents, we can ensure that talents aren't wasted and potentials are realized. Additionally, our communication with one another becomes gentler and more compassionate, instead of being full of judgment from our own blind spots. For me, CliftonStrengths©has gifted us what I like to think of as "The Language of You".

This is the first book in the series, Practical Strengths, a series of books dedicated to understanding the application and influence of our talents in our everyday lives. Future themes to be explored include: Careers, Communication, Goal Setting, Relationships, Recreation, Spirituality and Health and Fitness.

If you'd like to be informed of new releases and occasional updates, as well as download strengths-specific memes, additional workbooks, and have the opportunity to be a part of the future books by sharing your own story, please visit:

http://discoverjoself.com/resources

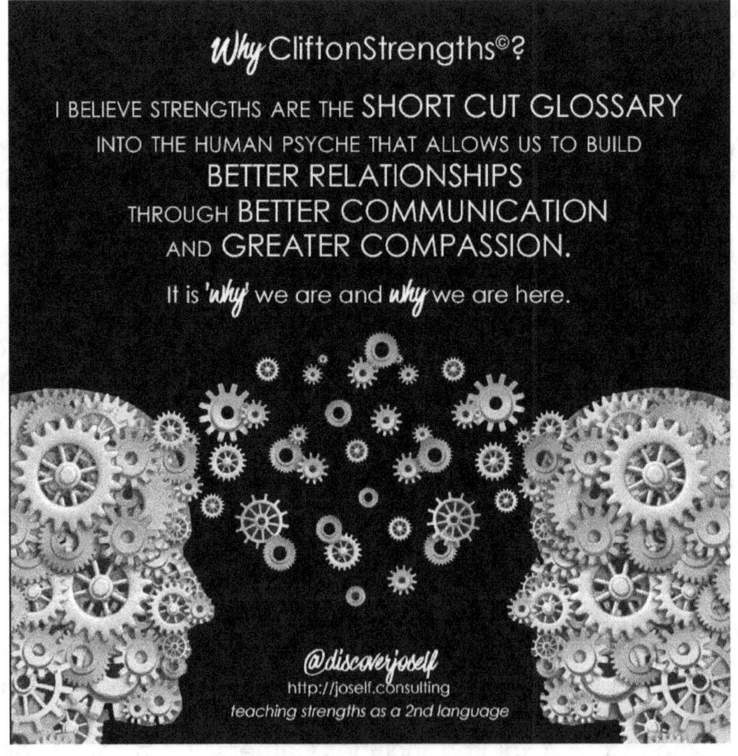

About the Author

Jo Self is on a mission to teach **CliftonStrengths©** as a second **Language.** She seeks to create a world where everyone can live to their full potential, talents aren't wasted, and happiness is contagious. As a single mompreneur and expat living in Peru, she understands the challenges and rewards that both entail. When she's not helping others create extraordinary lives, she can be found at the sewing machine, at the movies, enjoying a glass of wine with friends or horsing around with her terribly precocious little boy, affectionately known as O.

In the past, Jo developed nationally recognized and award-winning employee programs for Yum! Brands, the world's largest fast food restaurant company. And when she wasn't leading in-house teams to discover their strengths, she was on loan to other organizations helping them to do the same – all while serving on the national board of directors for her professional organization, ESM Association.

Once she left the corporate ranks, she started her own event business, Bon Vivant Savant, and was recognized as both a "Top Female Under 40" influencer in the community by Louisville Woman Magazine and also as a leading entrepreneur in the "40 under 40" list by Business Week Magazine.

After leaving the States and moving permanently to Peru, her entrepreneurial spirit continued with a tourism start-up that won a government grant as well as being recognized by ADEX as a top 50 start-up in the country. However, with all of these achievements, she still wasn't feeling fulfilled. A health scare in early 2015 set her on a course of self-reflection which brought her back to what she had always done best, had made her happy *and* given her joy. That answer was Strengths. She immediately contacted Gallup and began the journey for what she now confirms is her true calling, being a Gallup Certified CliftonStrengths© Coach.

Embracing her own strengths-based life led to the creation of her course, The Language of You. She guides other coaches and heart-based entrepreneurs to align their mission with their message, connecting them to their ideal clients. She also works with larger organizations to improve communication, leading to higher engagement and better relationships among team members.

"It is my deep desire to share with the world the power and gift that the CliftonStrengths language provides. It is the heart of this book series, Practical Strengths. I believe that sharing this language with one another leads to improving relationships through better communication and greater compassion for one another."

CONNECT WITH JO:

https://www.linkedin.com/in/joself/   http://discoverjoself.com

References

If you'd like to explore further:

<u>Assessments</u>

Strengths Explorer for kids ages 10-14
https://www.strengths-explorer.com/

CliftonStrengths© for Students for ages 15-21
https://www.strengthsquest.com/

CliftonStrengths©
https://www.gallup.com/cliftonstrengths/

(I do not make any profit from sharing these links above)

<u>My favorite books:</u>

StrengthsFinder 2.0 by Tom Rath

Your Child's Strengths by Jenifer M. Fox

Strengths-Based Parenting by Mary Reckmeyer

CliftonStrengths© for Students by Gallup

Please visit http://discoverjoself.com/resources for more information on books and assessments along with my guidance for how to get the most out of the materials.

www.ingramcontent.com/pod-product-compliance
Lightning Source LLC
Chambersburg PA
CBHW070805240726

48654CB00007B/217